Trombone

Easy Popular
Movie Instrumental Solos

Alfred Publishing Co., Inc.
16320 Roscoe Blvd., Suite 100
P.O. Box 10003
Van Nuys, CA 91410-0003
alfred.com

Arranged by Bill Galliford, Ethan Neuburg and Tod Edmondson

ISBN-10: 0-7390-4779-5
ISBN-13: 978-0-7390-4779-8

Contents

BELIEVE
(From "The Polar Express")

Words and Music by
ALAN SILVESTRI
and GLENN BALLARD

Moderately slow (♩ = 80)

COME SO FAR
(Got So Far to Go)
(From "Hairspray")

Lyrics by
SCOTT WITTMAN
and **MARC SHAIMAN**

Music by
MARC SHAIMAN

Moderately fast, with a strong back-beat (♩ = 160)

GONNA FLY NOW
(Theme from "Rocky")

By BILL CONTI,
AYN ROBBINS and CAROL CONNORS

5

Moderate rock (♩ = 192 or ♩ = 96)

28159

HEDWIG'S THEME
(From "Harry Potter and The Sorcerer's Stone")

By
JOHN WILLIAMS

IN DREAMS
(From "Lord of the Rings: The Fellowship of the Ring")

Words and Music by
FRAN WALSH and HOWARD SHORE

JAMES BOND THEME

By
MONTY NORMAN

28159

OVER THE RAINBOW

(From "The Wizard of Oz")

Lyric by
E.Y. HARBURG

Music by
HAROLD ARLEN

Moderately slow, with expression ($\bullet$ = 84)

28159

RAIDER'S MARCH
(From "Raiders of the Lost Ark")

By
JOHN WILLIAMS

THE PINK PANTHER

(From "The Pink Panther")

By
HENRY MANCINI

WAY BACK INTO LOVE

(From "Music & Lyrics")

Words and Music by
ADAM SCHLESINGER